The Great GiRaFFe ReScue

Saving the Nubian Giraffes

Sandra Markle

Millbrook Press • Minneapolis

For April Huyck–Panella and the children of Port Dickinson Elementary School in Binghamton, New York

Acknowledgments: The author would like to thank the following people for sharing their enthusiasm and expertise: Dr. Robert Aruho, Uganda Wildlife Authority, Kampala, Uganda; Jason Bredahl, Cheyenne Mountain Zoo, Colorado Springs, Colorado; Dr. Liza Dadone, Cheyenne Mountain Zoo, Colorado Springs, Colorado; Dr. Francois Deacon, University of the Free State, Bloemfontein, South Africa; Dr. Julian Fennessy, Giraffe Conservation Foundation, Windhoek, Namibia; Stephanie Fennessy, Giraffe Conservation Foundation, Windhoek, Namibia; Dr. Henrik Rasmussen, Savannah Tracking Ltd., Kilifi, Kenya; and Amy Schilz, Cheyenne Mountain Zoo, Colorado Springs, Colorado.

A special thank-you to Skip Jeffery for his loving support during the creative process.

Text copyright © 2023 by Sandra Markle

Millbrook Press™
An imprint of Lerner Publishing Group, Inc.
241 First Avenue North
Minneapolis, MN 55401 USA

For reading levels and more information, look up this title at www.lernerbooks.com.

Maps on pages 10, 19, 30, and acacia leaves icon by Laura K. Westlund.

Designed by Danielle Carnito.
Main body text set in Metro Office. Typeface provided by Linotype AG.

Library of Congress Cataloging-in-Publication Data

Names: Markle, Sandra, author.
Title: The great giraffe rescue: saving the Nubian giraffes / by Sandra Markle.
Description: Minneapolis, MN: Millbrook Press, an imprint of Lerner Publishing Group, Inc., [2023] | Series: Sandra Markle's science discoveries | Includes bibliographical references and index. | Audience: Ages 9–12 | Audience: Grades 4–6 | Summary: "After oil was discovered in Nubian giraffes' habitat, conservationists needed to move some of them across a river to safer territory. But there was no bridge and giraffes can't swim. Follow this unusual—and successful—rescue!" —Provided by publisher.
Identifiers: LCCN 2022020292 (print) | LCCN 2022020293 (ebook) | ISBN 9781728443218 (lib bdg) | ISBN 9781728485867 (eb pdf)
Subjects: LCSH: Giraffe—Conservation—Uganda—Juvenile literature.
Classification: LCC QL737.U56 M373 2023 (print) | LCC QL737.U56 (ebook) | DDC 599.638096761—dc23/eng/20220603

LC record available at https://lccn.loc.gov/2022020292
LC ebook record available at https://lccn.loc.gov/2022020293

Manufactured in the United States of America
1-50178-49822-9/12/2022

TABLE OF CONTENTS

A male (*front*) and female Nubian giraffe in Murchison Falls National Park. Nubian giraffes live only in Ethiopia, Kenya, South Sudan, and Uganda.

SOMETHING AMAZING!

Liza Dadone leapt from the truck as soon as it stopped. She waded into the waist-deep grass to get a closer look at a pair of giraffes in the distance. A veterinarian at Cheyenne Mountain Zoo in Colorado Springs, Colorado, Dadone was here in the wooded grasslands of Uganda's Murchison Falls National Park to work on a conservation project. She was part of a team helping endangered Nubian giraffes.

Easing close enough for a good look at the giraffes she had spotted, Dadone smiled. She recognized the male giraffe. He was the one the team had named Melman.

Researchers identify each individual giraffe by its unique-as-human-fingerprint spot pattern, which they record with a photo.

Dadone didn't need to check this male's coat pattern against the cataloged photos of Nubian giraffes to be sure of his identity. Although he was much taller and had matured from the two-year-old youngster she remembered, his quirky jaw shape was unforgettable. He was also part of the amazing story of how these giraffes came to be living here—on the other side of a river from where they used to live. That should have been impossible since giraffes can't swim, the river was too deep to walk across, and no bridge crossed the river. So how did these giraffes come to be here?

Giraffes are the world's tallest land animal. Males, which are taller than females, may stand 20 feet (6 m) tall.

START AT THE BEGINNING

The story starts in 2016 when Nubian giraffes living on the northern side of the Victoria Nile River in Uganda faced a crisis. Their already small population was in danger of shrinking drastically. So, what was causing this crisis?

Uganda's Nubian giraffe population didn't suddenly become in desperate need of help. All the different species, or kinds, of giraffes were facing threats. Giraffes roam wild only in Africa. And according to population surveys conducted by the International Union for Conservation of Nature (IUCN), the total number of giraffes living there dropped from more than 150,000 in 1985 to only 97,500 in 2016. For years, scientists and conservation experts had focused on helping Africa's shrinking elephant and rhino populations. They had not realized that giraffes were also suffering from the same problems. People were destroying giraffe habitats as they dug into the land for its natural resources or cleared it for farms, roads, and homes. Military activity and poaching, or illegal hunting, in and around protected wildlife areas were also killing giraffes.

Finally, after the 2016 population survey, scientists and conservation experts realized the giraffe population was shrinking enough to be concerning. Those remaining giraffes were scattered across twenty-one African countries, which made any attempt to help very difficult. And the total count was divided among the different species of giraffes. Although there were ongoing debates about how many species of giraffes existed, the problem was that too often male and female giraffes of the same species were cut off from each other. Those giraffes could not mate and produce calves, so the population of some giraffe species had severely decreased.

As far back as the 2016 giraffe survey, it was clear that Nubian giraffes in Uganda were facing a population crisis.

The problem for Uganda's Nubian giraffes was that almost the entire population lived in Murchison Falls National Park on the northern side of the Victoria Nile River. And in 2006, that was exactly the area where oil had been discovered. Preparing the land for oil well drilling would make the area unlivable for the giraffes. But years of political struggle over drilling rights in the park had prevented anything from happening until 2010.

The giraffe's coat pattern helps it to blend in where it feeds and avoid being spotted by prowling lions.

Then, through 2013, the Ugandan government allowed only exploratory well drilling. Those explorations determined the parkland held vast, extremely rich oil reserves. For a few more years, plunging global oil prices stalled the possibility of starting well drilling. But, in 2016, the Ugandan government granted licenses for drilling and oil production to multiple international companies. Those companies began drafting plans for building the roads and pipelines that would support oil well drilling in 2017 with the goal of having oil production begin in 2020. The plan included drilling more than four hundred wells across the home range occupied by Uganda's Nubian giraffes.

Robert Aruho, senior veterinarian for the Uganda Wildlife Authority (UWA), which manages the national parks and wildlife reserves in Uganda, said, "It was a wake-up call for realizing that having nearly all our Nubian giraffes living in that one place was like having all our eggs in one basket. We knew we needed to move some of those giraffes [from the northern region of Murchison Falls National Park] to start new, satellite populations." Satellite populations are small groups of animals that live in a separate habitat from the larger main group. These populations can increase the number of animals in a species and decrease the species' danger of extinction. As early as 2015, UWA had realized they needed to start creating satellite populations of Uganda's Nubian giraffes. In 2016, with destruction of the giraffe's habitat about to begin, it was time to make that idea a reality.

UWA called on the Giraffe Conservation Foundation (GCF), a conservation group focused on helping giraffes, to partner with them. GCF's first job was to find the location to launch a satellite population of Nubian giraffes. But how would they know if an area of land somewhere outside where the giraffes currently lived in the park was a suitable home for them?

Murchison Falls National Park, Uganda's largest wildlife park, stretches over 1,483 square miles (3,840 sq. km)—an area a little bigger than the US state of Rhode Island.

Nubian Giraffe 101

To help these animals, scientists needed to understand what makes them unique.

OSSICONES
These are two hornlike bumps between a giraffe's ears. Males have larger ossicones, and they use them to fight for a mate.

EYES
A giraffe's eyes are large and so widely spaced that it can see behind itself without turning its head.

EARS
A giraffe's ears are large enough to catch even the quietest sounds. A giraffe can turn its ears to listen in all directions.

MOUTH
A giraffe has front teeth only on its lower jaw. The front of the upper jaw is a tough, hard palate.

NECK
A Nubian giraffe's neck is about 6 feet (1.8 m) long and weighs about 600 pounds (272 kg).

TONGUE
A giraffe's tongue is about 17 inches (43 cm) long.

TAIL
An adult giraffe's tail may be as much as 8 feet (2.4 m) long with a tuft of hair at the tip, which makes it a good flyswatter.

COAT
A Nubian giraffe's coat pattern stops at its knees.

FOOT
Each of a Nubian giraffe's four feet has a two-toed hoof about 8 inches (20 cm) long and 6 inches (15 cm) wide. Its kick can stop an attacking lion!

FOLLOW THOSE GIRAFFES

Before the Giraffe Conservation Foundation team started searching for a location to launch a satellite population, they wanted to understand where the Nubian giraffes roamed and spent time in their Murchison Falls habitat. Then the team could go to those areas to identify what kinds of plants the giraffes were eating there. The best site to launch a satellite population would be where the giraffes had a similar habitat with a familiar food supply.

GCF had been putting tracking devices on giraffes since 2000 to map their habitat use remotely. But there wasn't any available data about the giraffes living in Murchison Falls. So, the team decided to capture some of the park's Nubian giraffes and attach GPS tracking devices to track them.

GCF used harnesses to attach GPS tracking devices to giraffes.

The capture team approaches slowly so they don't startle the giraffes into running. Giraffes can run as fast as 35 miles (56 km) per hour.

GCF cofounder and codirector Julian Fennessy said, "Attaching a GPS tracking device to a giraffe takes teamwork." So, GCF assembled a team of drivers, animal handlers, and a wildlife veterinarian. Once they had acquired vehicles and capture equipment, the team went to work. Attaching tracking devices on multiple giraffes took several days. Each morning, the team started early before the day was really hot. Everyone piled into pickup trucks, which followed the lead veterinarian's land cruiser. Being tall, giraffes were easy to spot on the grasslands. As soon as a giraffe was targeted, the land cruiser slowly moved closer while the other vehicles hung back. Once within range, the veterinarian leaned out the window, aimed a tranquilizer gun, and fired. *Zzzzzzoomp!*

If the team was lucky, the giraffe struck by the tranquilizer dart just kept on browsing until the drug took effect. But more often the giraffe took off running. Then the chase was on. Bumping and swerving, the trucks and land cruiser plowed through the grass to keep up. Although it was a rough ride, the team stayed with each giraffe for the nearly eight minutes it took the tranquilizer to take effect. They had to—the giraffe's life depended on it.

An adult giraffe can weigh as much as 2,000 pounds (907 kg).

As soon as the giraffe slowed down, the trucks braked, and the members of the capture team leapt out. They ran to get ropes around the giraffe and stop it. The veterinarian approached as soon as the giant animal collapsed on the ground. The next few minutes were critical.

The giraffe needed a shot of a drug to reverse the effect of the tranquilizer. That was important because the tranquilizer not only stopped the giraffe from running, but the drug also slowed its breathing. So, as soon as the giraffe was on the ground, the veterinarian administered the reversal drug. Once that drug kicked in—and it happened quickly—the giraffe was fully alert again. Then the team had to hold the giraffe down.

While the giraffe was on the ground, the team measured the animal's body length, checked its temperature, and took blood and tissue samples that could be studied later. Next, the GPS tracking device was attached. Once the giraffe was released, the device would transmit the animal's precise location every hour. Each GPS device had an identifying number, so the GCF team could track each giraffe's travels on a map of the park.

GCF tracked both males and females. They learned, within the same area, males roamed more and spent longer periods in different places than females did. GCF also learned something surprising about giraffes from another tracking study they were conducting. Julian Fennessy said, "We put GPS tracking devices on four giraffes in northwest Namibia and straight away that showed us they moved as much as 60 kilometers [37 miles] in a day and traveled between river systems. Before we learned that, it was just assumed wherever giraffes lived, they stayed within a river system and never traveled so far."

Examining a giraffe and attaching a tracking device takes a team. Several people hold its neck down. Without being able to swing its neck for leverage, the giraffe can't stand up. Another person covers the giraffe's eyes and gently plugs its ears with wadded-up socks to mute the giraffe's senses and keep it calm.

The Connection between Giraffes and Trees

Giraffes need to eat lots of tree leaves, branches, flowers, and fruit. A single giraffe can consume as much as 140 pounds (63 kg) of food per day. They are the world's largest ruminant—an animal like a cow that chews, swallows, and partly digests its food. Then the muscles in its long neck push wads of cud (partly digested plant material) back up to its mouth to chew some more. Dadone said, "You can see the swelling of a cud ball travel back up the giraffe's neck. Next, the giraffe's cheeks fill up and it starts chewing, but only for ten to fifteen seconds. Then it swallows and the chewed cud goes back down to the stomach." This process repeats over and over. Giraffes spend so much time eating, ruminating, and traveling between food sources that they usually sleep no more than four hours a day. When they do sleep, it's rarely longer than a five-minute nap.

Although giraffes will feed from bushes, they prefer tall trees. To reach something near the ground, a giraffe must spread its front legs wide apart as it lowers its neck, a position that makes it more vulnerable to predators. But trees take twenty, sixty, or even hundreds of years to grow tall. That means when humans cut down trees or trees die from disease or long dry periods, there are no quick replacements.

Because its tongue is prehensile (capable of grasping), a giraffe can wrap its tongue around branches and pull off leaves to eat.

Giraffes depend on trees for food, but they help trees too. One way giraffes help trees is by pollinating them. They transport the powdery male pollen grains a flower produces to the female part of the flower so it can develop seeds. A giraffe feeding on a blooming acacia tree gets its head and neck covered with pollen. As the giraffe wanders, stopping at different acacia trees to munch some more, it spreads this pollen to the next tree's flowers. The pollinated flowers allow the acacia trees to produce seeds. The seeds will sprout and grow new trees.

Later in the season, giraffes also eat acacia tree seed pods. Then, as the giraffes digest them, the seeds' tough outer layer weakens. That makes it easier for a new tree to sprout after a seed is dropped on the ground within a giraffe's waste. And that poop acts as a fertilizer to help the young tree get a good start.

A giraffe's lips and tongue are tough enough that it can safely browse thorny acacia trees.

HOME NEW HOME

Julian Fennessy said, "Once we learned where the [Nubian] giraffes were spending time browsing in the northern part of Murchison Falls National Park, we studied the vegetation in those areas. And, when we looked, we found the same type of vegetation resources in the middle of the southern part of Murchison Falls National Park."

Based on their research, GCF recommended launching the satellite population in the southern region of Murchison Falls National Park. This area was far away from the planned oil well drilling, and it offered the same kinds of trees and bushes Nubian giraffes were already feeding on in their current habitat. Since this area was within the national park, the giraffes would also still be in a patrolled area guarded against poaching.

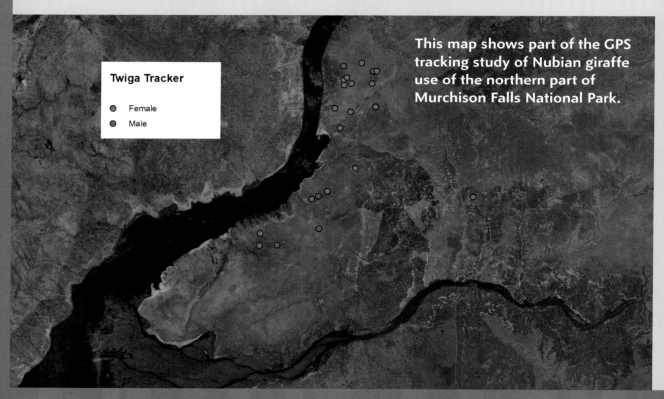

Twiga Tracker

○ Female
● Male

This map shows part of the GPS tracking study of Nubian giraffe use of the northern part of Murchison Falls National Park.

It was a bonus for the GCF team that the Victoria Nile River was too deep for giraffes to wade across so the river created a natural barrier. Once the giraffes were moved to the south side of the Victoria Nile River, they would be unable to go back to their earlier home range. But the river also presented the GCF team with a big problem. No bridge crossed the river. So, how could the Nubian giraffes be moved to a new location on the other side of the Victoria Nile River?

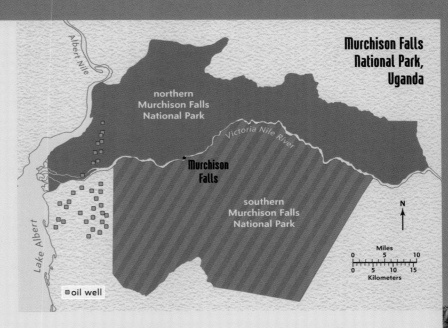

Murchison Falls National Park, Uganda

Albert Nile

northern Murchison Falls National Park

Victoria Nile River

Murchison Falls

southern Murchison Falls National Park

Lake Albert

N

Miles
0   5   10
Kilometers
0   5   10   15

oil well

The Victoria Nile River separates Murchison Falls National Park into northern and southern regions.

Where the Victoria Nile River pushes through a narrow rock cleft, it creates Murchison Falls.

OPERATION TWIGA BEGINS

There was only one way to translocate Nubian giraffes from where they lived in the northern region of Murchison Falls National Park to the southern part of the park. A team would have to capture some giraffes and load them onto a truck. Then the truck carrying the giraffes would need to be ferried across the river on a barge. It would be doable—but far from easy.

In 2016 the Uganda Wildlife Authority asked the Giraffe Conservation Foundation to continue their partnership and assist in capturing and translocating giraffes across the river. GCF agreed. It named the project Operation Twiga because *twiga* means "giraffe" in Swahili, one of the languages spoken in Uganda. Fennessy said, "We raised funds and bought the [transport] truck we'd need to move the giraffes. We also brought in expert capture people to train local Ugandans to help because we realized, if we're going to try this, we had to make the translocation successful."

Giraffes can't swim. Because of their long legs, short body, and long neck, giraffes initially float in deep water. Then they become unstable and go headfirst underwater.

Researchers learned there is no set time for how long giraffes stay with a group before moving on.

While observing wild giraffes, members of GCF had witnessed firsthand what other researchers had reported. Although giraffes are frequently seen in groups, they don't live in herds or even stick together as families. Codirector and cofounder of GCF Stephanie Fennessy explained, "In general we know giraffes have what is called fission [go apart] and fusion [come together] groups. That means they change groups and don't just hang out with the same group. The exception being we tend to see some females together a lot when all have young calves. Then they do something like a creche [nursery group] behavior where one or a couple look after the calves while others go and feed in more remote areas."

Because of the fluid social lives of giraffes, the GCF team was free to capture any giraffe it felt would be a good candidate for the new satellite population. So, the team planned to capture young adults because, being smaller, the young giraffes were a more manageable size to move. They also planned to move more females than males. That way there would be the potential for lots of calves to be born and expand the new population.

It was time for **Operation Twiga step 1: Capture the giraffes!**

The Operation Twiga team set up camp in the northern part of Murchison Falls National Park, close to an area where many Nubian giraffes were regularly seen roaming and browsing. And the team built a boma (b-oh-ma) there. *Boma* means "fortified pen" in Bantu, which is another language commonly spoken in Uganda. Captured giraffes would be kept in the boma to prevent their escape and to protect them from prowling lions.

Every day for two weeks, the capture team rolled out early in the morning in a caravan of trucks led by a veterinarian in a land cruiser. Some days they had to do a lot of driving to find young adult Nubian giraffes. Julian Fennessy said, "We chose them at random across the landscape and not just within one little area." GCF selected giraffes this way to avoid creating a population of closely related animals. Over time, when closely related animals produce young, any health problems are more likely to be passed on than with unrelated animals.

Once a giraffe was in the trailer, a tractor pulled it to Operation Twiga's campsite. That ride could last a few minutes or more than an hour, depending on how far from camp the giraffe was captured.

To everyone's surprise, when the team got an up-close look at one of the captured young males, they discovered he had an oddly protruding jaw. He was strong and healthy, though. Clearly, this feature had not kept him from eating. The team decided the young male's quirky looks should not keep him from being part of the satellite population. They named him Melman after a giraffe cartoon character. Melman quickly became an Operation Twiga team favorite because he was extremely calm and easy to handle. They hoped he would help keep the other giraffes calm during transport. So, Melman was among the six giraffes loaded onto the first truck headed to the satellite population site.

It was time for **Operation Twiga step 2: Translocate the giraffes!**

Because Operation Twiga was moving youngsters, multiple giraffes could stay together in the boma. Fights usually only happened when mature adult males were penned together.

THE BIG DAY

With the sun just rising, the caravan set off.
From the Operation Twiga camp, it was about 18 miles (30 km) to the river. While it was not a long distance, the transport truck had to drive *very* slowly to be sure the giraffes stayed steady on their feet. The only tense moment happened when Melman pushed his way around the other giraffes to look out each side of the truck. Fortunately, even jostled this way, every giraffe stayed standing. It took nearly two hours for the caravan of support vehicles and the giraffe transport truck to reach the crossing point on the northern bank of the Victoria Nile River.

During rough parts of the trip, team members hung onto the sides of the truck to call for a stop if Melman (*second from right*) or any other giraffes slipped.

The Victoria Nile River in Uganda flows some 300 miles (480 km) and is part of the Nile River system.

The only way for vehicles to cross the Victoria Nile River was on a barge. So, the Operation Twiga caravan had to be ferried across. Once the barge started, the trip took only about five minutes. The giraffes remained in the truck, but the people had to stand on the barge deck during the crossing. This was a safety measure in case the barge began to sink. Dadone, who was part of the translocation team, recalled, "I was nervous because I could see hippos and crocodiles in the water, so I really wasn't eager to go for a swim that day."

The park roads on the northern side of the river were regularly scraped and leveled. But when traveling away from the river toward the satellite population site, the roads were rugged, dirt trails through tall grasses.

Some of the giraffes fidgeted in the truck while on the barge. After all, the river crossing was a first for them. But Melman seemed only curious. Once again, he pushed his way from one side of the transport truck to the other. Stretching his long neck out, the young male looked this way and that while the barge chugged across the Victoria Nile to the river's southern shore.

Getting all the Operation Twiga vehicles and team across the river required more than one ferry trip. More than an hour passed before the team could begin traveling on land again. And on the other side of the river in the southern region of Murchison Falls National Park, the roads became rugged trails. The group had to travel even more slowly than before so the giraffes would stay steady on their feet in the transport truck. Finally, many hours later, the caravan reached the site chosen for the satellite population.

It was time for **Operation Twiga step 3: Release the giraffes!**

Operation Twiga team members shared smiles and snapped photos as the giraffes entered their new habitat.

To prepare for the release, the GCF team had visited the area days earlier and built a dirt ramp. The giraffe transport truck backed up to the ramp, and the team opened the tailgate. The giraffes were free, but they stayed inside the truck staring out. Melman, who was behind the others, shoved forward. Then the female at the front of the group lurched out of the truck and down the ramp. The other giraffes followed.

Those first six giraffes marked the official beginning of the satellite population.

Aruho said, "Watching those giraffes made me wonder 'Could we start satellite populations in some of Uganda's other national parks—those areas where giraffes once roamed?'" If that worked, Uganda would make sure no single issue, such as habitat destruction by oil well drilling, would ever again put the country's entire Nubian giraffe population at risk. But first UWA decided it needed to build up the satellite population in Murchison Falls National Park's southern region.

In 2017 the Uganda Wildlife Authority asked the Giraffe Conservation Foundation to partner with it on Operation Twiga II. GCF had already invested the time and effort needed to learn about wild Nubian giraffe behavior and their habitat requirements. And GCF had the equipment, trained team members, and the experience to successfully capture and translocate giraffes. So, they agreed to help.

It was time to start working on Operation Twiga II.

To give people easy access to the area, the government built more roads. But roads create increased risks for the giraffes living there.

TALL ORDER

Before 2017, remote GPS-tracking had played only a small role in supplying the GCF team with information about giraffe behavior. But that tracking data had provided valuable insights about where giraffes roamed and spent time within their habitat.

While the early GPS technology attached to giraffes had improved over time, Julian Fennessy had a new idea. He wanted a device that was small, lightweight, and perfectly shaped to attach to a giraffe's ossicone. Henrik Rasmussen, the managing director at Savannah Tracking, a company that makes tracking equipment for animals, was happy to create such a specialized device. The result is what GCF called the ossi-unit. It's solar powered, about the size of a standard deck of cards, and weighs about 6.5 ounces (185 grams). It attaches to a giraffe's ossicone with a bolt and straps.

The first ossi-unit was attached to a giraffe in 2017. The number being remotely tracked with ossi-units has grown annually, topping two hundred in 2020.

OPERATION TWIGA CONTINUES

Operation Twiga II translocated nineteen more Nubian giraffes—thirteen females and six males—across the Victoria Nile River to the same southern region of the park as before. But once Operation Twiga II was successfully completed, the Uganda Wildlife Authority decided to go beyond keeping all the country's Nubian giraffes in Murchison Falls National Park. Next, UWA wanted to start satellite populations in other parts of Uganda.

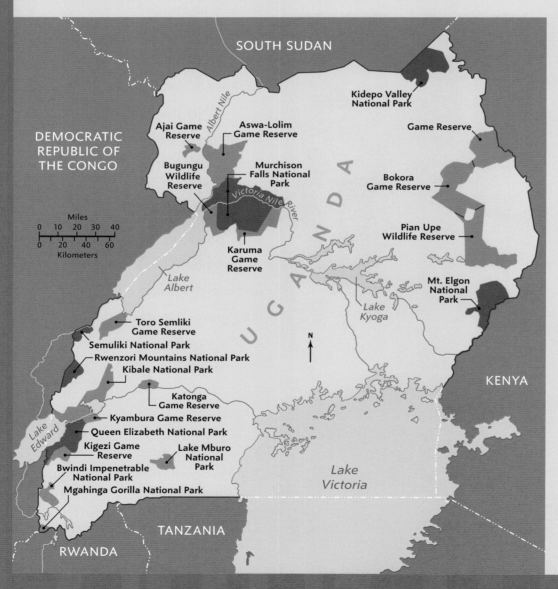

SOUTH SUDAN

Kidepo Valley National Park

DEMOCRATIC REPUBLIC OF THE CONGO

Ajai Game Reserve

Aswa-Lolim Game Reserve

Game Reserve

Albert Nile

Bugungu Wildlife Reserve

Murchison Falls National Park

Bokora Game Reserve

Victoria Nile River

UGANDA

Miles
0 10 20 30 40
0 20 40 60
Kilometers

Karuma Game Reserve

Pian Upe Wildlife Reserve

Lake Albert

Mt. Elgon National Park

Lake Kyoga

Toro Semliki Game Reserve

Semuliki National Park

Rwenzori Mountains National Park

Kibale National Park

KENYA

N

Katonga Game Reserve

Kyambura Game Reserve

Queen Elizabeth National Park

Kigezi Game Reserve

Lake Mburo National Park

Lake Edward

Bwindi Impenetrable National Park

Mgahinga Gorilla National Park

Lake Victoria

TANZANIA

RWANDA

Uganda has ten national parks and a number of wildlife reserves. Some of those areas are connected, offering the best possibilities for wild giraffes to roam and spend time with groups in different areas.

In 2018 Operation Twiga III translocated fifteen Nubian giraffes—ten females and five males—from the main population in the northern part of Murchison Falls National Park to Kidepo (keh-DEP-oh) Valley National Park. Wild Nubian giraffes still roamed in the Kidepo Valley. But that population had decreased to just thirty-five giraffes and needed more females to produce calves.

This time, moving the giraffes was an even slower truck journey. It took about ten hours and covered 300 miles (483 km) from Murchison Falls to Kidepo Valley. Along the way, the caravan passed through several villages, and people rushed to see the giraffes riding in a truck.

Kidepo Valley is Uganda's most isolated national park so two of the released females were outfitted with ossi-units to monitor where they roamed.

Whenever an Operation Twiga caravan passed through a village, people were excited to see the giraffes.

In 2019, for Operation Twiga IV, the Uganda Wildlife Authority decided to start a satellite population at a site in Uganda where there were currently no Nubian giraffes. They chose Pian Upe (pee-AHN OOH-pay) Wildlife Reserve because Nubian giraffes had lived in that area until the late 1990s. Years of military conflict had led to the giraffe population's decline and then eventual extinction in that area.

UWA teamed up with GCF yet again to translocate Nubian giraffes from Murchison Falls National Park to Pian Upe Wildlife Reserve. First, GCF studied the kinds of trees, bushes, and water sources in Pian Upe to choose the best possible release site. By now, the team was very experienced. It accomplished the capture, translocation, and release of ten Nubian giraffes—seven females and three males—within just two weeks. The team managed all that even though they had to battle through heavy rains that turned the roads to mud. The two trips they needed to make, moving five giraffes each time, each took sixteen hours.

In 2020 Operation Twiga V helped build up the new Pian Upe Wildlife Reserve population. Fifteen more Nubian giraffes—eleven females and four males—were translocated there from the northern Murchison Falls National Park population. That year, because travel was restricted due to the COVID-19 pandemic, a UWA team completed the operation on its own. It managed the work alone thanks to the previous years of giraffe capture and handling training from GCF.

With the completion of Operation Twiga V, Uganda was well into spreading out its Nubian giraffe population. The giraffes were no longer almost entirely in one location and vulnerable to whatever happened there. Even better, previously translocated female giraffes had given birth to calves. Aruho reported, "In March of 2020, GCF with the support of UWA did a [Nubian] giraffe population survey in Kidepo Valley National Park. Moving fourteen giraffes there just two years earlier had brought the population up to [almost] fifty [from thirty-five].

By the end of 2020, the survey [in Kidepo Valley] showed the population had increased to a total of sixty-two giraffes." As of 2022 the survey of the total Nubian giraffe population in Uganda was around 1,692 giraffes.

This group roaming in Kidepo Valley National Park is proof Nubian giraffes had made their new location home.

THE REST OF THE STORY

Dadone pointed out Melman to the other members of the team who were with her to check on the original Operation Twiga population. As she shared how he became part of Operation Twiga despite his quirky-looking jaw, everyone smiled because Melman wasn't alone. Usually, only the dominant male giraffe in an area had an opportunity to mate with the females. And becoming the dominant male required that male to win fights against the other males roaming the same area.

Later, upon hearing the team's report about Melman, Julian Fennessy smiled too. He said, "I think Melman being caught and crossing the [Victoria] Nile with Operation Twiga gave him an added bonus—less males to have to fight for mates. It's always nice to hear he's around and going strong."

Melman (*front*) is with a female giraffe. Male giraffes are usually only with females when they are seeking a mate.

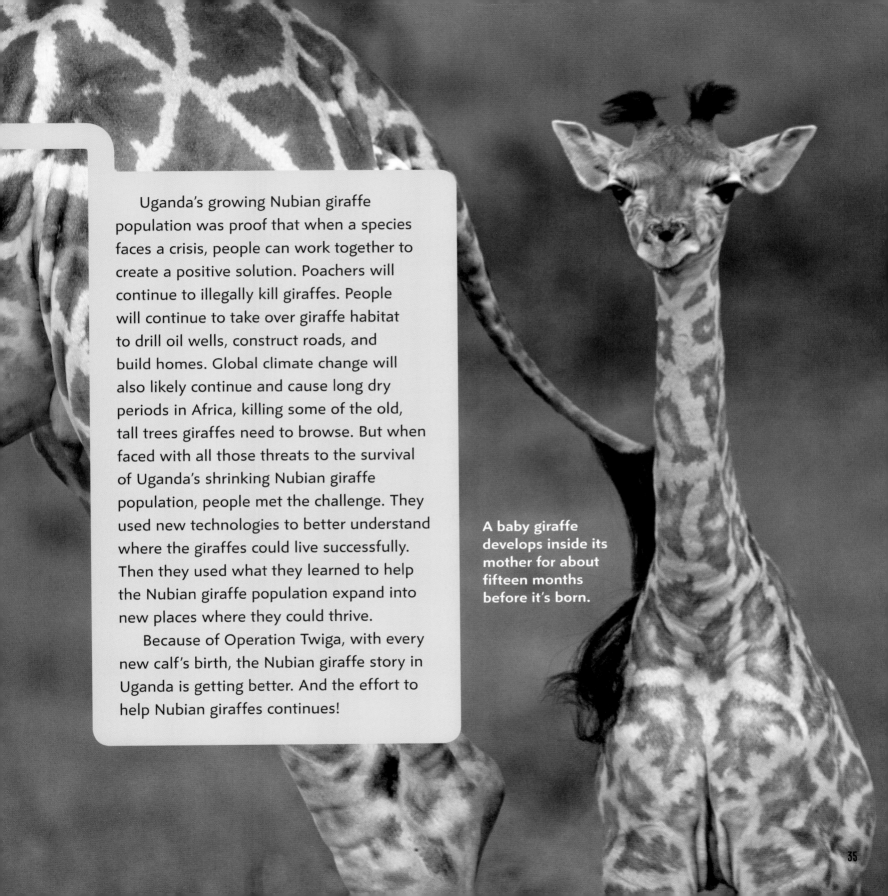

Uganda's growing Nubian giraffe population was proof that when a species faces a crisis, people can work together to create a positive solution. Poachers will continue to illegally kill giraffes. People will continue to take over giraffe habitat to drill oil wells, construct roads, and build homes. Global climate change will also likely continue and cause long dry periods in Africa, killing some of the old, tall trees giraffes need to browse. But when faced with all those threats to the survival of Uganda's shrinking Nubian giraffe population, people met the challenge. They used new technologies to better understand where the giraffes could live successfully. Then they used what they learned to help the Nubian giraffe population expand into new places where they could thrive.

Because of Operation Twiga, with every new calf's birth, the Nubian giraffe story in Uganda is getting better. And the effort to help Nubian giraffes continues!

A baby giraffe develops inside its mother for about fifteen months before it's born.

A Note from Sandra Markle

How did humans manage to not notice giraffes were slipping toward extinction? Julian Fennessy told me that, sadly, people only realize how important each species is to its ecosystem once that animal is gone. That could have been true of Nubian giraffes in Uganda if something hadn't happened to make people realize those giraffes were in trouble where they were living. But fortunately, that did happen before it was too late.

Years ago, while working on another book, I had an opportunity to climb to a high platform at a nature reserve, observe giraffes up close, and help feed them. I fell in love with those awesome giants. Learning Uganda's Nubian giraffes were on the brink of disaster sparked my investigation of the story. But it was discovering that organizations in Uganda and around the world were joining forces to help these giraffes that totally pulled me in. And Operation Twiga's building hope for a happy ending inspired me to keep digging to find out what happened.

That hope was driven home when I talked about Operation Twiga with Robert Aruho of the Uganda Wildlife Authority. He shared with me his delight in spotting the very first giraffe calf among the first satellite population. In fact, he told me seeing this calf was such a beautiful, hope-filled experience that he took his three daughters to see the result of the *big* challenge he had helped tackle.

May there be many more such hope-filled experiences for Nubian giraffes—for all giraffes. Their ecosystems need them. I don't want to imagine the world without giraffes!

Did You Know?

Even though a giraffe's neck is really long, it is like a human neck in that it has only seven vertebrae. But each of the giraffe's neck bones is about 10 inches (25 cm) long. Each is also a ball-and-socket joint, like the human shoulder, so a giraffe's neck is very flexible.

All but the very back of a giraffe's tongue is blue black. Scientists believe that the color keeps the giraffe's tongue from getting sunburned during long periods of sunny-day browsing.

A mother giraffe gives birth standing up. Her calf drops about 5 feet (1.5 m) to the ground. The fall doesn't hurt the calf. The hard landing helps it take its first breath.

It's a misunderstanding that giraffes don't make any sounds. Julian Fennessy said, "Giraffes make lots of different noises. They make everything from hums, snorts, grunts, and snuffs to roars and low frequency sounds. Giraffes just don't make noise regularly."

Glossary

browse: when a plant eater feeds on leaves, fruit, and soft shoots

calf: a young giraffe in its first year of life that stays with its mother and depends on her milk

climate change: major long-term changes in expected weather patterns

ecosystem: a community of living things that interact with one another and with the nonliving things, such as soil, water, and air, within their environment

endangered: a species that is seriously at risk of becoming extinct

extinct: a species that is gone forever

habitat: the natural home environment of a plant or animal

land cruiser: a kind of four-wheel drive vehicle used to drive over rough terrain

Nubian giraffe: originally called Rothschild's giraffe in honor of naturalist Lionel Walter Rothschild, who first described it in the early 1900s. It was also called Baringo giraffe and Ugandan giraffe. It was believed to be a subspecies of the northern giraffe. But in 2016, scientists decided this kind of giraffe was its own distinct species and changed its name to Nubian giraffe (*Giraffa camelopardalis camelopardalis*).

ossicone: one of a pair of bony parts on a giraffe's head, which is covered with skin and hair, and although it looks like a horn, it isn't one. At birth, ossicones are soft cartilage, like human ears, and lie flat against the head. After about a week, the ossicones unfold and, over time, harden from the tip down until they fuse to the skull.

poaching: illegal hunting

prehensile: a body part, such as the giraffe's tongue, that can wrap around something to grasp it

ruminant: a kind of animal that brings up its cud (globs of the plant material it eats) to chew again

satellite population: a small group of animals that lives in a separate habitat from the larger main group

species: one kind of living thing

tranquilizer: medication that slows bodily functions, causing loss of awareness. This is usually injected into a giraffe with a dart fired from a dart gun.

translocation: the capture, movement, and release of animals from one place to another

Source Notes

9   Robert Aruho, interview with the author, January 20, 2021.

13   Julian Fennessy, interview with the author, March 10, 2021.

15   Fennessy.

16   Liza Dadone, interview with the author, January 14, 2021.

18   Fennessy, interview.

20   Fennessy.

21   Stephanie Fennessy, interview with the author, May 12, 2021.

22   Julian Fennessy, interview.

25   Dadone, interview.

28   Aruho, interview.

33   Aruho.

34   Julian Fennessy, interview.

37   Fennessy.

Find Out More

Berkes, Marianne. *Over in the Grasslands: On an African Savanna*. Nevada City, CA: Dawn Publications, 2016.
Learn about animals that share Africa's savanna grasslands with giraffes.

Britannica: "Know about the Efforts of the Ugandan Wildlife Authorities to Protect Rothschild Giraffe"
https://www.britannica.com/video/193354/giraffe-conservation-plight-Rothschild-newscast-CCTV-Uganda-2016
Watch a short video about the Ugandan efforts to protect the Nubian giraffe.

Cheyenne Mountain Zoo: Giraffe
https://www.cmzoo.org/news/archive/cheyenne-mountain-zoo-welcomes-baby-girl-giraffe-calf/
Meet the Cheyenne Mountain Zoo's giraffes. Two live cameras on this website let you watch the herd when they're outside during the day.

Giraffe Conservation Foundation: Fun for Kids
https://giraffeconservation.org/2021/04/16/nature-workbook/
This is a fantastic workbook full of activities to learn more about ecosystems, food chains, and conservation efforts to help all wildlife, including giraffes.

Marsh, Laura. *Giraffes*. Washington, DC: National Geographic Kids, 2016.
Amazing photos bring this introduction to giraffes to life.

Index

Photo Acknowledgments

Image credits: © Musiime P. Muhebwe, pp. 1, 11, 13, 14, 15, 20, 22, 23, 24–25, 26, 29, 32; © Giraffe Conservation Foundation, pp. 4, 5, 11, 18, 21, 24 (right), 27, 31, 34, 35; Juergen Ritterbach/Alamy, pp. 8–9; Colin Seddon/npl/Minden Pictures, p. 16; Fernando Quevedo de Oliveira/Alamy, p. 17; ASUYOSHI CHIBA/AFP/Getty, p. 19; Nick Greaves/Shutterstock, p. 28; Jake Lyell/Alamy, p. 33; Skip Jeffery Photography, p. 36; znm/iStock/Getty Images, p.37.

Cover: prill/iStock/Getty Images; mxmvm/shutterstock.